COMPUTER PIONEERS

Ada Lovelace

First Computer Programmer

Amy Hayes

PowerKiDS press.

New York

Published in 2017 by The Rosen Publishing Group, Inc.
29 East 21st Street, New York, NY 10010

First Edition

Editor: Caitlin McAneney
Book Design: Mickey Harmon

Photo Credits: Cover, pp. 1, 3–32 (background) yxowert/Shutterstock.com; cover, p. 27 (Ada Lovelace) https://en.wikipedia.org/wiki/Ada_Lovelace#/media/File:Ada_Lovelace_portrait.jpg; p. 4 NYPL/Science Source/Getty Images; p. 5 Syda Productions/Shutterstock.com; p. 7 Richard Westall/Getty Images; p. 9 (inset) https://en.wikipedia.org/wiki/Anne_Isabella_Byron,_Baroness_Byron#/media/File:Annabella_Byron_(1792-1860).jpg; p. 9 (main) https://en.wikipedia.org/wiki/Ada_Lovelace#/media/File:Miniature_of_Ada_Byron.jpg; p. 11 https://commons.wikimedia.org/wiki/File:Carpenter_portrait_of_Ada_Lovelace_-_detail.png; p. 12 https://en.wikipedia.org/wiki/Ada_Lovelace#/media/File:Ada_Byron_aged_seventeen_(1832).jpg; p. 13 Linda Steward/E+/Getty Images; p. 15 (main) vovan/Shutterstock.com; p. 15 (inset) https://en.wikipedia.org/wiki/William_Frend_(social_reformer)#/media/File:William_Frend.jpg; p. 17 https://upload.wikimedia.org/wikipedia/commons/1/17/1895-Dictionary-Phrenolog.png; p. 19 https://en.wikipedia.org/wiki/Charles_Babbage#/media/File:Charles_Babbage_-_1860.jpg; p. 21 traveler1116/E+/Getty Images; p. 23 https://en.wikipedia.org/wiki/Analytical_Engine#/media/File:AnalyticalMachine_Babbage_London.jpg; p. 25 DEA PICTURE LIBRARY/De Agostini Picture Library/Getty Images; p. 27 (inset) https://en.wikipedia.org/wiki/Ada_Lovelace#/media/File:Diagram_for_the_computation_of_Bernoulli_numbers.jpg; p. 29 https://en.wikipedia.org/wiki/Ada_Lovelace#/media/File:Ada_Lovelace.jpg; p. 30 naihei/Shutterstock.com.

Library of Congress Cataloging-in-Publication Data

Hayes, Amy, author.
 Ada Lovelace : first computer programmer / Amy Hayes.
    pages cm. — (Computer pioneers)
 Includes bibliographical references and index.
 ISBN 978-1-5081-4830-2 (pbk.)
 ISBN 978-1-5081-4767-1 (6 pack)
 ISBN 978-1-5081-4810-4 (library binding)
 1. Lovelace, Ada King, Countess of, 1815-1852—Juvenile literature. 2. Mathematicians—Great Britain—Juvenile literature. 3. Calculators—History—Juvenile literature. 4. Computers—History—Juvenile literature.
 I. Title.
 QA29.L72H39 2016
 510.92—dc23
 [B]
                              2015025358

Manufactured in the United States of America

CPSIA Compliance Information: Batch #BS16PK: For Further Information contact Rosen Publishing, New York, New York at 1-800-237-9932

Contents

A World Without Computers

Computers are an important part of everyday life. They include phones, tablets, and laptops, which are used for work, play, and communication. Computers are used in every field, from medicine to the military, and there's a specialized **computer program** for just about anything.

Try to imagine a world without computers. There would be no video games and no social media websites. If you wanted to look something up, you would have to find a book. If you wanted to write something, you would have to grab a pen and paper.

Ada Lovelace grew up in a world where computers didn't exist, yet she went on to create the first computer program. Ada Lovelace broke barriers to help us understand these tools we now use every day.

Ada Lovelace

Thanks to pioneers like Ada Lovelace, computers help people access information almost instantly. They've revolutionized the way people learn and communicate.

Unusual Parents

Ada Lovelace was born Augusta Ada Byron in London, England, on December 10, 1815. She was the daughter of Anne Isabelle Milbanke and the famous poet Lord Byron. Her parents were very different from one another. Anne Isabelle was strict, religious, and very focused on academic studies. It was very unusual at the time for women to pursue education, because it was considered unattractive and even dangerous. However, Anne Isabelle, also called Lady Byron, loved thinking about the world around her and especially enjoyed math.

Lord Byron, on the other hand, was one of the world's first celebrities. He was brilliant, emotional, and wrote beautiful poems. His poetry made him famous, and he traveled often and attended wild parties. His wife hoped she could bring some order to his life.

Lord Byron was an important writer of the Romantic Period, which was an artistic and literary movement that began in the late 1700s in Europe and put emphasis on strong emotions. Byron's work is still read today.

Early Years

Ada's parents weren't married for very long. Their differences soon tore them apart. Anne Isabelle separated from Lord Byron and took Ada with her when the baby was only a month old. It was the last time Ada saw her father.

In the first few years of Ada's life, her grandmother raised her. Different nursemaids looked after her at her grandmother's house. Her mother traveled a lot. However, Lady Byron made sure Ada was cared for properly.

Ada's mother wanted to give her the best education she could have. Lady Byron wanted to make sure her daughter would be calm and **logical**. She worried Ada would turn out like her father. Lady Byron was determined to make sure her daughter would be ruled by logic and not emotions.

Ada, age 4

Lady Byron was a strange woman for her time. She was highly educated, but had odd views on raising children.

9

A Different Kind of Imagination

When Ada was a young child, Lady Byron noticed her daughter liked to imagine things. Ada would pretend to be an adult, as if she were playing house. This worried Lady Byron. She didn't want Ada to make things up, even if it was just a game. Instead of encouraging Ada to use her imagination, Anne Isabelle Byron instead decided that she would fill Ada's head with math.

By the time Ada was five, she was learning the basics of **geometry** and could add together sums of five or six different numbers. Lady Byron hired the best tutors she could find for her daughter. When Ada was six, she had a **routine** every day that involved learning arithmetic, grammar, spelling, reading, geography, French, drawing, and music. Her favorite subject was geography.

Lady Byron hired the best tutors, or private teachers, she could find for her daughter.

The Importance of Math

One day, Ada wrote in her journal that she didn't like math. When Lady Byron read this, she became very upset. Lady Byron believed math was very important, and she wanted to make sure Ada believed the same thing. Lady Byron made Ada go back into the journal and rewrite the entry. Ada wrote a new entry apologizing, saying she would work harder to make her mother happy. From that day forward, Ada worked hard at math.

At age seven, Ada was doing well in all her subjects. The one-on-one tutoring ensured she had the best education. Ada's bright mind was soaking up every ounce of knowledge she could find. Her genius was just beginning to show.

Ada worked one on one with different tutors. Many rich children had governesses who taught them in their houses. It was like homeschooling, except there was a paid professional working in the house.

A New Tutor

When Ada turned 13, she had learned just about everything her tutors could teach her. It was at this time that Lady Byron enlisted her former tutor, Dr. William Frend, to continue Ada's education. Frend had a sharp mind, but was shunned for his religious beliefs as a **Unitarian**.

Ada and Frend started writing letters back and forth about astronomy and **algebra**. Ada began asking him very theoretical mathematical questions. "Theoretical" means that she could imagine concepts without seeing them in the real world. Frend didn't agree with theoretical math. For example, when Ada questioned him about negative numbers, he simply said they couldn't exist.

Though Ada's quest for knowledge quickly outgrew what Frend could teach her, the two wrote letters back and forth for several years.

Dr. William Frend was a talented astronomer who encouraged Ada to go out and look at the stars. Unfortunately, she was a very sickly young girl and was temporarily **paralyzed** from a bad case of measles during her correspondence with him.

Taming a Wild Mind

Lady Byron had a difficult personality. She was very loving, but could be controlling. She accepted nothing but excellence from those around her. She sheltered her daughter from life in London and only allowed Ada to associate with Lady Byron's own friends. She was very worried that Ada was going to lead the wild life Lord Byron had led. Imagination was discouraged, and Ada had very little contact with people her own age.

Instead, science and math were Ada's friends, and they helped keep her mind on practical things. At age 18, Ada wrote to her doctor, "I find that nothing but very close [and] intense application to subjects of a scientific nature now seems at all to keep my imagination from running wild."

Lady Byron became obsessed with **phrenology**. It assumed you could tell if a person was good or bad by the shape of their head. Lady Byron only allowed Ada to associate with people who had a certain head shape. Phrenology was later disproven.

Babbage and the Difference Engine

When she was 17 years old, Ada "came out" to society. This means she could officially be chosen for marriage. She met many people and went to many parties. During this time, she met Charles Babbage.

Babbage had been working on a machine he called the Difference Engine. It would be able to perform basic arithmetic functions, like a calculator. The government funded his research, which was extremely advanced for the time.

The Origin of the Difference Engine

One day, Charles Babbage and his close friend William Herschel were checking mathematical tables for the Royal Astronomical Society. They kept finding errors. Frustrated, Babbage said, "I wish to God these calculations had been executed by steam," meaning he wished they'd been calculated by a machine. Herschel then challenged Babbage to make such a machine. The quest to make the first calculator would take years, and Babbage would never fully complete it.

At Babbage's house, he had a model of the Difference Engine, which he showed off to his guests. Many were impressed with this machine that seemed to think on its own. However, few inspected it further. Ada was fascinated. She looked all over the model, examining the gears, rods, and wheels until she figured out how the machine worked.

Charles Babbage

The British government funded Babbage's Difference Engine with the hopes of being able to easily calculate the paths of their navy's ships.

Continuing Her Education

In Europe in the 1800s, women were discouraged from learning. It was considered strange if a woman was well educated. However, this didn't stop Ada. Her thirst for knowledge was growing stronger. However, it was difficult to be taken seriously by the men in her field. Lady Byron considered her options and picked the perfect tutor to continue Ada's education.

Mary Fairfax Somerville was a respected scientist. Even Lady Byron, with all her strict standards, approved of her. Ada looked up to Somerville as an inspirational figure because of her intellect and determination to learn. Somerville often took Ada to lectures at King's College, London. One lecture was on Babbage's Difference Engine. This renewed Ada's interest in the machine.

Mary Fairfax Somerville worked hard to become an accomplished astronomer and mathematician despite her parents' and her first husband's dislike of educated women. She was one of the first women welcomed into the Royal Astronomical Society.

Mary Fairfax Somerville

Mary Fairfax Somerville was a Scottish mathematician. As a young girl, her education was unorganized, and she ended up attending only one year of formal schooling. She started learning algebra by accident. Sources say that she noticed strange mathematical symbols inside a woman's magazine. Others believe she discovered them in one of her brother's math books. Either way, she was interested in what the algebraic equations meant, which lead to a lifelong study of math and science.

The Analytical Engine

In 1834, Babbage abandoned the Difference Engine in favor of a new machine called the Analytical Engine. It would be a programmable computing machine. The British government refused to fund this engine until the Difference Engine was completed, but Babbage found funding in other European countries. He began working furiously on the engine, but most of his work was highly theoretical.

While the Difference Engine would merely compute necessary numbers, the Analytic Engine could do something called conditional branching. This meant that rather than entering many different numbers to get a desired answer, the machine could compare results in order to focus on getting an answer faster. The Analytical Engine would be the first mechanical computer.

Conditional Branching

Conditional branching is an important part of computer programming today. An easy way to talk about conditional branching is to picture a line on a graph. The Difference Engine could determine different dots on the line, but conditional branching would be able to determine the shape of a line. For example, if the line curved, what would be the highest point? A Difference Engine could figure this out after lots of trial and error, but the Analytical Engine would provide the answer much more quickly.

The Analytical Engine

The Analytical Engine was eventually constructed and now sits in the Science Museum in London, England.

An Article on the Engine

In 1840, Babbage gave a lecture on the Analytical Engine in Turin, Italy. Luigi Federico Menabrea, a young military engineer from Italy, heard the lecture and was fascinated by the device. He decided to write a paper describing the Analytical Engine and how it worked. Two years after the Turin lecture, Menabrea's article was published.

A close friend of Ada Lovelace's, Charles Whetstone—a scientist known for his experiments in electricity—asked if Ada would translate the article from French into English. He knew Ada's superior understanding of math and French made her the perfect person for the job. When Babbage found out Ada was translating the article, he suggested she write a new one instead. However, Ada declined, saying she would just add notes to the original article.

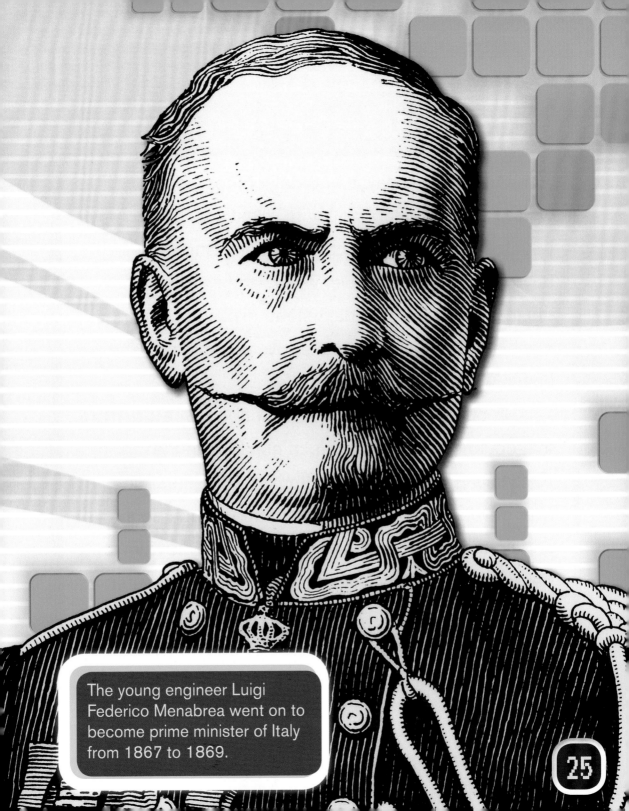

The young engineer Luigi Federico Menabrea went on to become prime minister of Italy from 1867 to 1869.

25

The First Computer Program

Ada worked day in and day out for months, writing letters to Babbage with questions, adding any updates he had made to the machine. She went far beyond the original article, which explained only how the machine worked. Ada instead explained what the machine did, what practical applications it had, and how it would be used.

In one of her notes, Ada described an **algorithm** that could calculate a series of numbers in the Analytical Engine. This algorithm was the first one ever developed to make a computing device do a certain task. Today, we call that computer **software**. For that reason, Ada is known as the first computer programmer. She even imagined **radical** new uses for the machine beyond what Babbage had come up with.

In the end, Ada's notes ended up being much longer than the article she translated. This longer, translated article appeared in *Scientific Memoirs* in August 1843. She signed her name A.A.L., so people wouldn't know she was a woman.

Diagram for the computation by the Engine of the Numbers of Bernoulli. See Note G. (page 722 et seq.)

Ada's algorithm

Ada's Lasting Impact

Ada Lovelace wrote the first computer program over a century before the technology was created to use it. Babbage's machines lay unfinished, to be completed by later generations, but Ada's programming was correct. Her imaginative uses for his machines still impact computers today. She even believed that computer-generated music and graphics would be the wave of the future.

In her honor, one of the very first programming languages was called Ada. In the 1980s, Ada was the language used to control the United States' most powerful weapons. It's hard to believe that Ada and her contributions were almost lost to history. Now, every October 13, we celebrate Ada Lovelace Day, which honors women in science, technology, engineering, and mathematics.

Ada Lovelace died shortly before her 37th birthday, but her discoveries have lasted lifetimes.

Timeline

December 10, 1815:

Ada Lovelace is born Augusta Ada Byron.

January 1816

Anne Isabelle Byron leaves her husband and takes Ada with her.

1824

Lord Byron dies. Ada grows up knowing almost nothing about her father.

1829

Ada becomes very ill. Because of Lady Byron's strange medical beliefs, she is bedridden for the next three years.

1833

Ada meets Charles Babbage for the first time and examines the Difference Engine.

1834

Charles Babbage begins work on his Analytical Engine.

1835

Ada marries William King.

1838

Ada's husband becomes the Earl of Lovelace. Ada receives the title "The Right Honourable the Countess of Lovelace."

1842

Luigi Federico Menabrea publishes his paper on the Analytical Engine.

1843

Ada translates Menabrea's paper and writes the world's first computer program. She goes to great lengths to explain how such machines will change the world. Her predictions later prove true.

November 27, 1852

Ada dies of cancer at the age of 36.

Glossary

algebra: A kind of math that involves letters representing number variables.

algorithm: A set of steps that are followed in order to solve a mathematical problem or complete a computer process.

computer program: A set of instructions that are performed on a computer.

geometry: Math that deals with points, lines, angles, shapes, surfaces, and solids.

logical: Having to do with sound reasoning.

paralyzed: Unable to move.

phrenology: The study of the shape of the skull based on the belief that it can tell mental abilities and character.

radical: Very new and different, not ordinary.

routine: A regular way of doing things in a particular order.

software: Programs that run on computers and perform certain functions.

Unitarian: A member of a religious group that stresses individual freedom of belief, the use of reason in religion, and a united world community.

Index

Websites

Due to the changing nature of Internet links, PowerKids Press has developed an online list of websites related to the subject of this book. This site is updated regularly. Please use this link to access the list: www.powerkidslinks.com/compio/ada